Land and Sky

Poetry from the heart of
Cat S Ginn

Land and Sky

This book is dedicated to my husband, Jimmy, our children, Landon and Skye, and my mother, Faye; who continued to believe in me, even when I didn't.

...

He's my Land, he is calm,
heals earth's edges, then moves on
rocks my world with his palms-
he's my saving, healing balm

She's my Skye, azure she,
she illuminates my sea
Steady rolls- onward home-
she's my beauty, my life's dome

Land and Skye; they are mine
they're my precious peace, sublime
Different, same, none to blame
He's my potion- she's my flame-

Without Land, without Skye
I know I would wilt and die
Couldn't run, couldn't fly
How I love my *Land and Skye*

For Landon and Skye

Spring

...

So sing the springs beneath the falls,
as water drips and drops from walls,
when after rains each robin calls
to summer waiting 'round the bend

When gentle breeze amongst the trees
sets loose a sway, begins to tease
that tension left from winter's freeze-
that bitter chill you fear won't end.

As slowly rises, morning's sun,
to kiss the dew left graced upon
each wondrous blade of grasses grown
which glints and gleams then slowly sends

up to the atmosphere each day
sweet mist of moisture, come what may;
renews the earth as if to say,
"I'm here as promised, let's begin!"

...

I rise to meet
the morning mist
push back the urge
to lounge,
resist--
I'll stretch long limbs
then climb outside
this warm cocoon
in which I hide
My yawn gives way to dawn
at last
as light falls
on this great crevasse
Into it, eagerly,
I slide
deep down inside
this great divide
No one I know
has known me well
enough to read
my heart which tells
I long to live
in sights,
pristine,
'midst lizards,
toads,
and all that's green

'til I should draw
my final breath
to leave this world
'neath cloak of death
I'm sure more beauty
I'll not see
as such beneath
these lovely trees

...

What's it like to be the rain?
Falling up from splashing down
A simple drop of falling rain
Raining down upon the ground

Falling up from splashing down
Wets the flowers and the grass
Raining down upon the ground
Sun comes out to shine at last!

Wets the flowers and the grass
Someone tell the sun to shine
Sun comes out to shine at last
Heaven smiles on us sometimes!

Someone tell the sun to shine
Tell the moon to wait his turn
Heaven smiles on us sometimes!
Moon and stars will have to learn

Tell the moon to wait his turn
A simple drop of falling rain
Moon and stars will have to learn
What it's like to be the rain.

...

As springtime melts the month of May,
the summer rains in, pelting June;
in sheets of wet it shears off clay,
sure seems the floods have come too soon.

The lakes and rivers protest, rise,
it seems the earth has much to say!
The mouth of Brazos opens wide
as springtime melts the month of May.

The great blue herons, egrets too,
stay still 'neath shelters long past noon;
awake to thunder, lightning cues,
as summer rains in, pelting June!

The water moccasins will swim
and float downriver 'most the day;
torrential downpours won't give in
as sheets of wet soon shear off clay.

The wood ducks duck past bobbing branch
beneath an amber harvest moon;
as cattle graze, they stomp, then scranch-
sure seems the floods have come too soon.

...

There's an ebony girl
seeking freedom in the night
she lives in the soles of my feet
She raises pink palms to the heavens, singing psalms,
I know she and I will be free

There's a bent Jewish man
who is older than the trees
feeding pigeons in the park as he coos—
and the wisdom that he brings
to the flock as he sings
is the same he rains down as good news

There's a homely white girl
who longs to be touched
she wraps herself and rocks on bended knees
She'll take heed in her need to fertilize life's seed—
she and I, we are one and the same

There's a wise Asian Buddha
sitting by the pond
speaking to the frogs and the leaves
He will sing to my soul
on cool breezes, humming low--
I know I am him
and he is me

There's a Cherokee that cries in the night, by and by
as the heavens open up to take heed
He and I, we are one
for our journeys have begun
much the same, we are flames—

we both bleed

I am you
you are me
we're the same
can't you see?
No matter what the color of our skin.
From a seed we are grown
raised to walk boldly on
'til our paths meet as one at the end

...

I sit in the bright light,
watch you sprout-
from the side of a rock
while all about you
dead grass grows
but, you don't care...

I want to be there.

While a cool breeze blows,
it whips you about,
you're a burst of spring
in a wintered sprout;
there's so much in you
that without a doubt...

I want to share.

So, I raise my chin
to the warmth of the sun,
soaking in that strength,
take it in on the run...
'cause I know some stuff
has just come undone-

but, I'm not sure where.

When I look back down
I see, it's arrived-
a visitor
from a neighbors hive-
though you're a weed

in a great big yard-

I'm so aware...

that, in the scheme of life
we all are made
strong enough
to be someone's shade,
to be that life force-

and that's ok...

we all need to care.

So I'll be your weed
with your nectar, sweet…
though I might be tired
and dead on my feet-
there's a southern breeze
making life complete-

you're in my everywhere.

...

I found a ladybug today
amongst the shower streams
it played
in rivulets of azure rain
then bellied up
and sang my name

It sang to hummingbirds outside
a lilting tune it carried high
among the weeping willows, bare
there it sat and tarried where
a robin red and breasted swell
took all those notes
and sang them well

Then, telling grackles flying by
that I was there and standing by...
while breeze blew east
and then to west
the robin's red and poofed out chest
fluffed feathers misty from the rain
began to sing my song again

And once the clouds took all those tears
they'd held for me for all those years
they started to release them all
and then, the rain began to fall

as water soaked into the land
the flowers clapped with joyful hands
to see the weeping willow smile

(that's not happened in quite awhile)

Now, when the willow smiled, I swear
the sun peeked out of clouds up there
and wondered what was going on
just who was singing joyful songs

By now the world began to sing
But, I will tell you one more thing
I've never seen such joy, so smug…
as in that little ladybug.

...

As morning breaks on the meadow
the baby doe pauses to stare;
a silence broken in shadow,
she wonders, is anyone there.

A breeze blows softly around her
as the grasses sway to and fro;
each blade about her, she'll feel stir,
as morning breaks on the meadow.

Soft light falls gently in patterns,
seeps through leaves to play on her there;
she stops... she listens, and then turns...
the baby doe pauses to stare.

It's times like these you can hear earth
if you stop and listen, you know?
To hear when beauty just gives birth—
a silence broken in shadow.

Just take a break from the discord
a moment of silence or prayer
to hear the doe as she whispers
and wonders, 'Is anyone there?'

...

Here amidst a sprinkled blanket-hue
A bluebonnet parade is overdue
This spring, they sprung up overnight it seems
To dot the countryside and make it gleam

In waves of periwinkle topped with white
They'll wave their caps and stagger in full sight
No flagstone pillar near will weigh them down,
They just move forward, on, then homeward bound

Fence posts of cedar, stripped and bared for rails
Will stretch horizons 'cross bluebonnet trails.
Barely fenced, they kept none in or out...
Grackles roost or squirrels just sit and pout.

Acres left and acres right, no home...
Miles and miles to elsewhere linger on
You'd wonder why they put a boundary there
In such wide-open spaces, who would care?

Wave, bluebonnets, hold your vigil fair-
Sway, bluebonnets, in the Texas air-
Nowhere else on earth are you this free...
Dance Bluebonnets, do-si-do with me!

...

Wisteria still grows on vines out back
though twisted, gnarled it still on lattice, climbs;
according to the Farmer's Almanac,
it should be 'death by frost,' a thousand times!

Yet every year, come Spring it grows again,
no matter that she's dead now, twenty-five...
each year she springs eternal, my Maxine-
and like a phoenix rises as she thrives!

And though it's just her memory exposed,
yes, Spring reflects the love that we once shared;
and I'm reminded when the sweet breeze blows,
Maxine is gone, for I'm the one who's spared.

If I live only one more Spring 'twill be,
another chance her spirit blows through me.

...

The journey of the dragonfly
leads onward, westward, home;
its webbed wings weave through grass, through leaves,
where e'er it wish to roam.

While wild, it waves its wings so free,
seems brash, without a care-
without a doubt, it flies about-
empowered by fresh air.

If only I could really fly
among the trees with birds...
but, I'm content as they fly by
to soar so high with words.

...

Round up the dragonflies,
round up the bees,
sing to the robins that fly through the breeze.
The trumpets are blooming out on the vine-
they're large and they're orange
and they're looking so fine!

Call to the butterflies,
call to the trees,
tell the roadrunners and drop to your knees.
The trumpets are blooming out on the vine...
they've blown and they've grown
and they're one of a kind!

Look to the azure skies,
look to the seas,
hear the wind beckoning, calling for me

The trumpets are blooming out on the vine;
they cling to the spring-
they're yours and they're mine!

...

I remember your face that day, as radiant as any movie star,
as any precious stone. You twirled with such grace, as
layer after layer of crinoline, satin and lace raced about
your feet and ankles. Your tiny, slender hands delicately
woven amongst the folds, you swished and swayed,
sashaying your way across the pebbled path and into his
heart.
Behind you, that background of scarlet fronds rises to the
sky where they are met with chartreuse splatters of
blossoms which need no mention-- you are the center of the
universe! Scattered at your feet, tiny Black-eyed-Susans
dance along the trail behind you—

I smile to myself, straighten your portrait, and…wiping one
lone tear, wrap my arms about cold shoulders… turn off the
light, and wonder if you're happy tonight.

...

Maybe God is the man in the moon
Shifting tides, blowing wind
Causing storms and monsoons...
Healing souls with the sun
As the Earth slowly moves
Is he our guidance? Will he be here?
Even when darkness ensues?

In the night, without sleep
I wonder at it all- would the earth
In its majesty- without the moon-
Just fall?
Would the sun shine so brightly
To burn our tender skin-
Or would we fade away
And this cycle begin again?

Without the moon above,
Would the night owl find its way?
Or would it cower in the darkness,
Until the light of day?

Would the fierceness of the winds
Blowing across the land
Wash out and destroy this host
Of merry men?

It's a mystery, I must admit
One I think they'll never solve
I'll just add it to that list:
Like, "Did we all evolve"?

But, on nights like this
I look up from life's cocoon
to find comfort up in space
by that face in the moon.

Summer

...

She loves going barefoot,
  each step that she takes
  another step closer to earth.
    She walks with her head high,
    her heart open wide,
    she's searching for more than just dirt.

Her soul had intended to honor the sky,
but found she was led by the land.
  It matters not whether her toes sink in sand,
  or tether to creek beds which lie
  so lazily, crazily, winding their way
  through forests; she speaks to the trees!

    Until you have touched
    bare feet to life's sod,
    you've really not been to your knees.

...

Blackberry cobbler
on ugly orange dishes.
Kumquats grown out back
while my wishes
fly through the air
on a salty sea breeze...
   These are the best of my memories.

Knobby knuckled hands
roughed up from hard work;
a full-bodied woman
not afraid to unearth
veggies from the garden
while down on her knees—
   These are the best of my memories.

Hands folded, neatly
on an apron on her lap;
head rested back
in her chair for a nap...
Cotton dress down to her
earth-worn knees...
   These are the best of my memories.

...

Where poppies grow 'neath Texas skies,
awash in crimson, sable eyes-
they sway together, honestly
amidst the breeze, beneath the trees.
Where poppies know, the robin flies.

Then, way above, and circling high
it dips and swirls, comes flying by,
to sweep so deeply by the sea
where poppies grow.

Like Flanders Fields, brave men do lie
beneath the warmth of Texas sky-
this blanket grows so you can see
the blood they've spilled for you and me.

Their spirits live in poppies' eyes
'neath Texas skies.

...

Amidst the thorns a flower grows
to spread its petals wide;
its lovely face tilts up and shows
her golden sunny side.

Though hidden in the desert here
where not much grows to see,
they give us something we hold dear;
a blooming rarity.

For though they're few and far between,
in places hard to cope...
and desolation grips this land,
the cactus rose brings hope.

...

The blazing sun sets low tonight
as branches, cursing, cry for rain.
Without it, trees will suffer blight;
decline in strength- and start to wane.

Horizon flickers with the heat,
absorbing every joyful bleat-
as cattle limp, the live oaks wilt
upon earth's continental quilt.

...

I lie beneath a summer's slivered moon,
above me float past memories of life;
as sighs escape my lips I think of you,
as music plays sweet tunes on drum and fife.

I fell asleep as springtime just came round
and gave myself to you a might too soon...
made love, ourselves, upon the grassy ground;
to lie beneath a summer's slivered moon.

If there's one thing in life I thought I knew,
it's how to free myself from daily strife;
but I'm afraid I don't know what to do,
above me float past memories of life.

Just lie with me and watch the stars tonight
the clouds change shapes, as we must often do.
Constrictions always seem to be too tight...
as sighs escape my lips I think of you.

If I could have one wish for you and I—
one thing come true to last for all our life—
I'd be right here with you until we die,
as music plays sweet tunes on drum and fife.

...

In saffron breeze I close my eyes
against the warmth
of Texas skies
soft, silky wind traces my skin-
I lean in.

Tangerine clouds close languid lids—
isn't this
how heaven is?

From here and there,
upon the air, a hummingbird
flits and flutters in…

there he is again, upon the wind;
pretends caress upon my dress…
shifts against my knee
in gentle tease…

I close my eyes…
in saffron breeze.

…

Wait…
Did you hear that?
It was subtle…
just ever so slight
A sound heard in the darkness,
in the crevasse of the night!

A creaking… A groaning,
a moaning if you will
Of the loons on the lake,
and a crying whippoorwill

If you've heard the loons crying,
you'll wonder just why
they cry in the darkness
and let out a long sigh

It's the long lonely moan
that the bullfrogs will make
on the west end of the bank
of the mossy, sage lake…

If you listen closely
in the sweet, lithe night
you'll hear crickets prancing
with all of their might
You will hear their legs scratching
and the scritching they make
on the lost, lonely shore
on the secluded side of the lake

When you listen closely,
to the humming birds hum
as they beat their wings softly
like the drumming of drums

On a soft summer's night
they've a melody all their own
In their feverish humming flight
you can hear them scurry home

If you put it all together
a sweet symphony plays
In the breathless nights of summer…
in sweltering August days

...

A dandelion... summer's breeze
sweet older pup, down on her knees;
those blooming flowers; honeybees

...such shorter lives have these.

A walk with someone that you love-
that perfect fitting baseball glove;
a talk with Grams or God above,

...some things we all dream of.

Sweet puppy's breath, a baby's cry,
proud tears of joy in mother's eyes;
your children's love for which you'd die;

...these things you cannot buy.

Recaptured memories of you;
you met someone, and I did too-
and suddenly, at once, I knew...

...our dreams have all come true.

...

Sweet breezes play a melody,
as darkness comes, I'll sing along;
west winds will whisper merrily,
for I have traveled far and long.

When morning comes to find you here--
devoid of pain, devoid of fear--
aware at last, love, you're the one
who calms my fire to set my sun.

...

The *Mighty Oak*, strong in its stance,
stands hard in its tracks, never sways,
does not dance.
Never budging, never bending,
never moving at all...
But the mightiest, of the mighty...
can he fall?

When the *Wind*, in her sweetness,
plays with the trees,
She dances, and prances, and teases his leaves,
she'll woo and she'll ask him, "Come hither... come
please"
For that's how she treats
the trees....

But the *Wind* when she's angry, she'll bite and she'll hit
and believe me the *Tree* will know
It's been bit!
And the *Tree*, unbending, will come
crashing in, if only
it had bent in the wind.
There's a tree by the river, which breathes
in the air and lives
on the river, for the water is there.
Her name is *Mother Willow* and she's grand
as you please!
Simply, the most forgiving
of trees.
For she sways and she sways

in the breeze as it blows
and she bends and she rustles
as the *Wind* moves her so…

Her feet stay rooted to the ground
but her branches, they dance all around!

So sway with the *Wind* if it moves you to be
Forgiving of things in life that you'll see
For you just never know,
you might need to be
      a *Willow which bends in the breeze.*

...

A storm's blowing through
as the water's rising high;
I'm still missing you,
and the old dog's fine-
there's a mist on the lake
as I'm drinking my wine-
  life's turned azure blue.

There's no other place
that I'd rather stay,
when you're here with me,
or you're far away;
for the calling of the loons
means my heart's okay-
  life's turned azure blue.

Have you seen the trees
when the leaves turn up?
Have you heard the rain
when you're falling in love?
Have you ever been down
and you can't get enough?
  You might be azure blue.

I'll turn to the sky
'til I see your face;
when the night birds sing
I'll look for a trace
of the mist on the lake
when I'm drinking my wine-
  'til I'm azure blue;
    there's a storm blowing through...

...

In great expanse where the buzzards fly
along beside the roads we drive
where westward sun licks azure sky
the mountains rise the clouds still thrive

Along beside the roads we drive
from east to west across hillsides
the mountains rise the clouds still thrive
where lies a golden road beside

From east to west across hillsides
imagination creeps along
Where lies a golden road beside
we'll travel merry, sing our songs

Imagination creeps along
the vastness opens minds and hearts
We'll travel merry, sing our songs
no need for maps or plotted charts

The vastness opens minds and hearts
where westward sun licks azure sky
No need for maps or plotted charts
in great expanse where the buzzards fly

...

I root to the soil of my safety,
In the sun,
I will stretch to the sky—

My arms I will flail
to the heavens for warmth;
as I brown all the parts that are pale.

A glow that lies rooted inside me,
as a youth is new life,
it bleeds free—

Yet, as Winter races 'round me
I notice...
That Spring returns slowly to me...

In my Summer I'm a willowy, wild one
my roots are dug deeply 'neath me-
It may take a gale force
to snap my strong hips... but once done,
it will break my esprit!

In the Fall, I return to the Earth,
and the Earth returns me to seed...
But for now, my young arms, so green and so strong--
stretch over my body so free!

. . .

A legacy looms all around us
and the core of my beating heart knows
This may not be how the earth found me
but it's how a legacy grows!

From the roots of the ones
before me, who have
lived and have shared
with us, words—
We can't ignore they explored
ground and bared the seeds,
then died to have themselves heard!

Put your ears to the earth
you will hear them-
as they whisper their legacies deep,
into soil they have toiled and lie
buried in;
now into that which they seep

...

When she loves a poem,
she holds it at arms' length
and, with her thumbs and forefingers,
it succumbs to soft edges,
lingers on ledges of her self peace

as thoughts and sounds release,
easing out 'esses,' making messes--
as thoughts of small miracles
coalesce--
    ah yes, but I digress.

When she loves a poem she takes it home,
soothes it down to sleep,
keeps it under pillows
to billow softness from inside places;
filling nature's spaces- touching and tracing
lines on the faces of childhood friends-
    on subtle winds.

When she loves a poem
she loves it from the inside;
longs to take flight with wings,
sings to the tops of trees
with ease...
    caressing tails and turning dresses
    with each whip of the wind--
        and she'd do it again
        for a friend...

When she loves the poem it rises with luster,
fills the sweet breeze, tosses and turns,

then yearns to be free.
So sweetly and demurely it rides
by her side...
then, glides with a whisper,
to her feet by moonlight.

...

In fairness to all others, I should say,
there's never been more beautiful a bride
than you-- who moves the earth with just one sway--
oh how you rule my heart, I'm mystified!

Yet, even winds which toss about the sea
and build so monumentally as storms,
have never had the same effect on me
as seeing your sweet smile; oh how it warms!

But, like the ocean waves will swell and rise,
you too, sashay away without a glance;
and soon you'll spread your wings and take to flight,
to live your fairytale in sweet romance.

As parents we must face our loss alone...
a casualty of one more stepping stone.

...

I'm sitting in the gathering dusk
the sound of waves,
smell of musk…
a husky roar
above the rush
of whooshing winds.

I sit alone, watch the tide,
it ebbs and flows…
I can't abide, one more hello,
one last goodbye;
I miss you so.

I watch the moon with Venus lie
while on its back
in pale moonlight;
the air escapes my lips as sighs,
the night rolls by.

I close my eyes… I'll never sleep;
too many memories
I want to keep.
At last the tired begins to seep
into my bones.

I sit amongst the gathering dawn;
I know we're through, still time ticks on.
The rushing waves,
still rushing on—
Still rushing on...

...

Redbud blooms
in bright sunlight
skein of geese
    take flight-
        garble by-

road runner stops
with his tail held high
    looks left-
        then right-

stretches out,
        flies—

Texas sun
shines my way-
    cornflower skies
        on a cool March day

so many thoughts,
not too much
to say-

I miss your eyes.

...

Remember when we used to sit and talk
on backs of hay trucks in the midst of Fall?
I still remember how you used to balk
at sitting on that dirty hay we'd haul.

September came and went so fast it seemed,
we'd spend our days in beds of trucks on bales;
we still thought 'out' was nothing more than dreams-
and someday we might take to seas 'neath sails.

But hopes are born on backs of dragonflies,
those wings of wispy wonders fly right past.
Still, if you dream too long, that hope soon dies,
you'll find the ones you have-- they just won't last.

So put your hand in my hand, follow me...
we'll make each one come true; dream carefully!

…

If you listen to oceans, you will hear him
As he frolics in waves and on sand

If you go to the mountains, you may see him
Where he hikes over hills, 'cross the land

Sit still in the forest where you feel him
There he'll run as he barks, and he'll play…

When you kneel to the earth, take comfort in this
These are the ways he will stay

...

I sit in warm sun rays to soothe my soul,
as birds flit, flutter by
I'm feeling whole...

Though March has just begun
the air is mild
and somewhere deep within me
there's this child who longs
to run and just feel free-
soothe and salve the wounds
to complete me.

If I had just one wish
I guess it'd be...
you'd be just as warm
and feeling free.

...

When life gets too harsh
Loud, tears stinging-
I seek out nature and its peace

With no dings or pings or rings to beckon me
I'll sing to the trees
On knees soiled from soul searching,
The earth plants me
Roots to my core
The animals and trees, they nourish me
And I am both one with god

And separated from man
Sustained enough
To toughen my exterior
Remain superior
And walk on my own

Full grown

Atone for the harsh
That I've put forth
March myself back to reality
And just be

Fall

...

Butterflies and bees
aloft on a breeze
visit the leaves
of Rosemary
Though late in the year
they flutter near here
beseeching the blooms
of Rosemary
They flit and they fly
among Susan's eyes
right past them to be
near Rosemary
Her blooms softly swoon
though it's way past June
she reeks as they seek
sweet Rosemary
Her scent in the air
they'll swoop down to share
the pink-purple songs
of Rosemary
November's soft chill
just can't break their will
they're tossing their kisses
to Rosemary
Though frost may come soon
it just cannot ruin
the love they bestow
on Rosemary

...

I fancy me that yellow tree
shimmering leaves in windy breeze-

saffron she stands
badly sawed
pretending she is all
those amber and kelly greens are—

even as she preens,
seems to be as free
as any tree
upon the hill,

so still.

She fills the spot
she's got

She even fought with rotted limbs
just to get a glimpse
of Spring's surprise;
Susan's eyes
black as dots
attack the glen.

Then,
when the day
is through
she drops her yellow leaves
sleeps through

winter's cold
till spring brings blossoms true
amidst morning dew

and
I'm renewed-

that's what that yellow tree
would do.

...

Among the forest where I used to play
The leaves are gone, it's autumn here
In the bed of the forest where I used to lay

No squirrels, not even birds or deer
Have graced this place since early spring
The leaves are gone, it's autumn here

A chill in the air, Mr. Winter brings
Around our heads up in the air
From somewhere else we hear birds sing

A raccoon lumbers on without a care
At early dusk the moon will shine
There's a magic in the frigid air

But the chill before is left behind
Magical moments creep up with the dark
Stars rush past on their way through the night

On this enchanted journey on which I've embarked
Among the forest where I used to play
Magical moments creep up with the dark
In the bed of the forest where I used to lay

…

Oh! Autumn,
soothe us in splendor
Touch each treetop
Oh, so tenderly…
Tip the tops of twilight fading…
wanton, wistful,
woozy, persuading
all my fancy, so beguiling,
leave me bashful but, still smiling…

Oh, dearest Autumn,
touch me sweetly
tease each leaf to blaze completely…
Woo them all until they shiver,
turn to gold,
then drop upriver…

You'll leave lithe limbs
in fascination!
Leaves say thanks
for their own cessation!

Hail Autumn!
We Fall in praise as we receive
these Winter days!

...

Grackles grack 'midst live oak trees
in August shade, which Texas needs;
as morning sun bears down,
    Earth pleads for rain.

Its plain- refrains and shatters forth
from months of thirst, its face turned North
in search of cool winds to freeze.

On knees, diseased, inquietude, frothing since June,
its thirst for moisture often rude...
    wilts and waves in subtle winds,
    while longing just to drink again
    as baby birds screech beaks to sky-
        vultures fly low by.

...

We fell into Fall
as we gazed at the trees
In gratitude, bowing,
we fell to our knees

Their splendorous colors
like susurrus flames
In crimson and scarlet
and golden they wave!

Then just when the colors
have cloaked them in style
The rain claims their dresses
and leaves them in piles

Inspiration: "Then came the rain undressing the trees of their Autumn finery"

-PL Plumley

...

Today I rounded that first cul-de-sac, and
as I came loping down Sundance, the sun caught the fall
leaves after a light rain—
The trees glistened, renewed, as I was, by the moist, clear
air—

All was good with my soul.

In that instant, I forgot everything and remembered my love
for flying—
pushed harder, feet to pavement, Blue October in my head
—pressed on,
heart pumping,
lungs expanding,
soul fed...

and I ran.

...

Indigo sky
meets amber rose ridge,
where time slips away
and night falls in-
as slivers of a moon
resting sleepily on its back…
westward in the sky
sets my mood-

relaxed.

Bare maple branches-
sticky-stark toward hues,
streak past ambers and roses
leaving blues…
as Canadian geese
in fours
and then
twos,
honk happily past
leading thoughts
toward you.

...

I'm seeking rainbows way up in the sky,
from animal balloons that float on by.
Their patterns mix and mash along the way
in puffs of stuff which make them seem okay.

Beneath them, rolling hills create a view,
which must seem quite sublime to honored few.
Serene in solitude, 'neath patterned skies-
too bad sometimes the earth, in silence, lies.

For nothing is as perfect as it seems
and candy clouds don't last from childhood dreams.
But for the moment I'll believe it's true
and close my eyes to only think of you.

If there's one thing I know of life and art-
perfection is a place inside your heart.

…

As Autumn leaves start blazing
bewitched by
October's woo—

amber is praised so amazingly
before orange turns to rust
then ecru

But the fire from the flames
of sweet scarlet
warm my soul for Decembers
to come

It segues a soft breeze
as it swishes through trees

Winter's embers softly
glow inside me

...

I long to take your hand to lead you home
To where you're safely cared for, not alone
Yes, where your heart can mend and beat with ease
I long to make you well from this dis-ease

To soothe your setting suns so you will know
Each time you lay your head upon pillows
That morning time will bring to you a breeze
And always know your heart will beat with ease

So follow me, my friend, stay close to me
Walk with me awhile and you will see
That never will you ever walk alone
So come, I'll take your hand, I'll lead you home

...

In gingham skirts of petal pink
with roses on the hem,
I twirled through trees that towered tall-
a flower on a stem.
My arms stretched wide to greet the sky,
my face turned t'ward the sun;
I ran barefoot, beneath soft clouds,
a young girl on the run.

In autumn's glow, life's undertow
soon swept me out so fast...
and all those daisy days we played,
we soon found wouldn't last.
The shadows cast by pine trees there
flashed lines across my face,
till summer's sun, like childhood's done,
was gone without a trace.

I sometimes see Mom standing there,
her smile, a fading light;
but when I try to reach for her
she disappears from sight.
But still, I'll spread my arms real wide
and close my eyes to dance;
just wishing she was by my side,
I'll take a backwards glance.

...

I want to be the only name
you whisper in your need
From the rising of the sun
to the crash upon your knees

From the calling of the loons
upon your dying bed
I want to leave my kiss
upon your fevered head

When sands of time cease shifting
upon the ocean floor
Fountains turn away man's wishes
and will receive no more

The clouds will spill the balance
of all their grief renewed
to wash away those sands of time
so life begins anew

Though we may never hunger
as we have hungered when
the taste of love has seared our lips
to satiate and blend
Begins to warm and mend our hearts
as we will coalesce
Then time can heal our aching souls
for we've been truly blessed

As darkness seeps around us
and gathers at our feet

closing over all we love
we'll surely not be beat
Though lonesome melancholy
may echo life's refrain
when sands of time will shift our way…
you'll whisper back my name

…

I stare at the old man standing beside the creek. Fall has come to the hills of the Ozarks. Morning frost settles early in the hours before coffee, bacon, and loose-beaked birds, who enjoy tapping their tiny toes on the gutters along the roofline by my bedroom, are even awake.

Long before that, Daddy Fred wakes up, takes his coffee cup and stands beside the creek... listens to the sounds of morning. In those sounds, which echo in his yesterdays and give him hope for tomorrow, he'll see her—hear her; and even smell the cookies she bakes, wafting past on a breeze. When he's out here like this in the mornings, every morning, he'll catch a glimpse of her; that four-foot-eleven-inch frame of hers, always slight and agile. Even past one hundred years old, she can still lithely hop the fence to chase chickens, piglets, or a stray fox that might come along.

Now, standing here among the sounds of tree frogs, whippoorwills, and crickets, beside the rushing water of the Missouri creek, Daddy Fred and Great-Grandma Silvy both disappear like the apparitions they are; leaving me with only my memories-- the ones I choose to keep.

fallen leaves rain down
from bitter winds sweeping through
my family tree

...

Every once in awhile something threatens
to break inside me
Part ways with reality and rise, unchecked,
To spill into the atmosphere,
creating charred bits and jagged pieces...

If I can, on occasion, meld with nature, set bare feet to soil,
fingers and toes to water—
I am grounded in a way which can only be explained to
those who feel the same.

Pick up a smooth stone, skip it in water,
and feel the ripples smooth out your hard edges

...

He gasps as she breathes out the last breath
of her day with a sigh... oh my;
gives it gracefully... willingly
he inhales gratefully

It's a ritual- a realistic happening
which dawns daily
nightly they're tethered tightly, tenderly-
mending raw edges- smudging jagged edges
of each other's faces
filling spaces where lost pieces of
life's puzzles
jig out of jagged holes
in their souls

It's a process, each moment spent
a lifetime-
each nighttime
mending bent bumps
in their carapaces- holding spaces
touching faces, kissing places
no one else sees—

with tender ease,
appeasing, pleasing, and
painting over chipped
hurt...

It works.

For over thirty years,
she melts fears, drinks tears
washes wounds
sings tunes to tug heartstrings

She sings
as he clings close
tugs deeply
sets fingers firmly, fastidiously
about arteries
pulsating portions reserved
for the living,
lying closely,
mostly just moved by the way
she grooves
no time to lose

She oozes love
he takes it in, and then,
turns a deeper shade of *Jade*.

...

There's a murder in the trees today;
a diabolical scheme.
A quest to rise
to azure skies
then plummet to the stream which runs
beside the house; makes haste,
becomes the waterfall.
There's a murder in the trees back there--

I can hear them call.

Black grackles sit upon my gable
cawing to the skies.
Flapping wings and doing things
with haunting, cackling cries.
As silence builds its chasm,
soon my interest,
piqued, will rise-
for 'midst the limbs sit all his friends,
with gleaming, yellow eyes.

Dusk falls across in shadows
felled by oaks which, wilting,
stand in solemn stillness; susurrus rustles
they creep in hallowed bands.
Then, rise above the cemetery,
a gnarled and menacing hand
points west to test the winds of change;
the murder still stands.

...

Fallen blossoms are so often
lying still
upon the ground.
Oh, so softly,
they drift loft'ly
as they scatter all around.

While inside, I hide securely,
search for cures to heal
my pain...
    fallen blossoms
    are so often
    kissed by mist
    of fallen rain.

...

Inside this space where no one comes but me,
I seek to calm myself so I can breathe.
In subtle beauty I wish to be imbued,
in shades of Fall, I long to be infused.

The air has lifted, I'm free now to be
an Autumn hue which falls about your feet.
So aptly named, the leaves will take their leave
of limber limbs, still, I can feel them grieve.

But don't despair, repair will come this Spring
when buds return and birds will all take wing.
They'll fly in skies of azure, billowed clouds,
as blossoms bloom where nature loves out loud.

I will, in secret, bow my head and pray
forgiving all, just thankful for this day
Still knowing, somewhere, I am meant to be
out here amongst the world on bended knees.

...

As curdled clouds close over August's moon
deep purple crevices of stone-cracked earth
seek shadows, softly, licking live oaks, hewn,
as moisture traps organic bursts of birth.

As man will measure minutely on life's
grand scheme, so too, trees seem the ones to fall,
yet man possessing much, his life so rife,
still can't surpass the earth or scale its heights.

But somehow, both live side by side and so,
must shelter one another through life's storms-
though some winds always try to conquer, blow,
respect and admiration help perform.

Accept the hand of someone, can't you see?
There's beauty all around you... follow me.

...

I sat in peace with solitude
in shrouded mist, my mood subdued;
as all my thoughts turned inward to
those nights with you, those nights with you.

While fog surrounds me nothing's heard,
no lap of water, flap of bird;
this echoed silence, so absurd-
still not a word, still not a word.

The times we had I would not trade;
much richer this, than accolades,
still in my head, these thoughts pervade...
I wish you'd stayed, I wish you'd stayed.

My solace meets with fortitude,
I find no reason to delude;
I rise within my soul, renewed...
sweet interlude, sweet interlude.

I wonder if you think of me
when you are touched with Autumn breeze,
will you sit often 'neath these trees?
With memories... sweet memories...

...

I heard the screaming of the trees next door
As the vilest of language flees from blades
--Thrust, cussed,
Clawed their way through--

Didn't you?

Yesterday--
the wind brought songs
As if we all belonged
Yet today,
I must say,
It all seems not right as the little bities bite
As sweet cedar perfume fills to brim
Both the skies
And my eyes

I hear the treetops fall--
Weird echoes
beseech us all
when the screaming of the trees
brings a forest to its knees
Leaves one man and a house, all alone.

Grief, full grown, echoes
in the falling of the trees

Winter

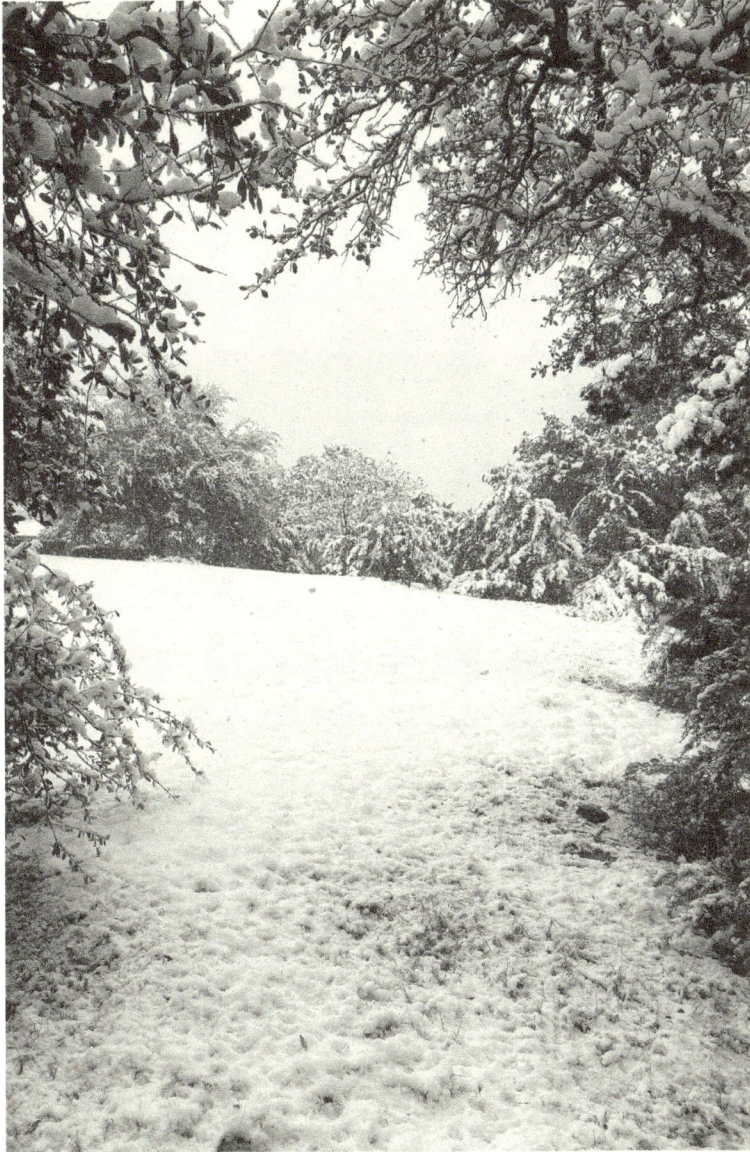

...

I'd like to be a drop of rain—
I'd fall to earth to ease your pain
I'd fall once then rise again
into a cloud then back to rain

Recycling life is what I'd do
turn to tears as I touch you
fall so softly on your cheek
to rise again from misty creek

Reform myself to touch another;
father, sister, baby, mother
Who should I touch?
Where should I go?
Who needs quenching?
        Do they even know?

I'll die a death to live another,
touch one hand
then touch another

Drench a field of wheat as I go
rise to air-- I'm making snow!

A little drop of rain, am I,
or just one tear you silently cry?

He was born in the winter
of his elderly snow
    amongst packed-up daydreams
    long since stowed.

She appeared through a window
her voice moonlit, it glowed-
    how was he to know?

She would enter him as moisture--
the dewdrops of his spring,
    emerging from the soil
    of his eternal upbringing.

She'd root in his beginnings
to splay to all his ends--
    touching nerves to fingertips,
    to where true love begins.

As summer came in waves of heat,
she swept right over him;
    he welcomed her as sunshine,
    and dove right in to swim!

They frolicked in waves of passion,
leaping grasses tall...
    she pooled about his feet
    as he just relished in her fall...

As winter rose about him
in the recess of his heart,
    where warmth would melt the ice
    from off his fireplace and hearth,

she saw, outside the window,
the falling flakes, and so--
    she knew the time had come for them
    to face his Elderly Snow.

She gathered all his daydreams
to lay by firelight…
    his journey now was ending,
    she never left his side.

As moonlight fell upon them
his spirit rose to go--
    she left through that same window
    by the fire's light of his Elderly Snow.

...

The reeds by the lake gently sway to and fro.
the ducks are leaving the pond now, we stop
to watch them go. The water freezes soon,
and soon it will snow...It's winter in the center
of her heart. We parted back in college, I
haven't seen her since. She married after
leaving to some guy who acted tense. I
didn't want to leave her, but I had to get
out fast, we parted, But that didn't last. She
stayed around her parents' place, a little longer
than she should. I told her she should get out
of there, out of the neighborhood. But you
never could tell her much, never could tell her
at all. So I stood there, and watched it all fall.
Her mother got sick, in the spring of her
migration. She was done... had two kids, and
a tubal ligation...Ran amok with a train guy,
got pregnant, then got high, That's when she
learned how to fly. And she flew to the moon,
on a bright summer's day, but she flew too close
and she begged them to let her stay. So they
locked her up tight (through a fairytale or two...)
and that's when she turned Baby Blue.
And she stayed Baby Blue for most of her life
Sky, if her day went well. Azure, if she cried.
And I sang her a song each time to dry her eyes...
but Azure is still blue, anyway you cry. Azure is
still blue, anyway you cry. Then, when the time
came to go she'd said her goodbyes. She'd taken
all her pills and swallowed them up tight. And she
waved them away, as she waved them goodbye as
azure was filling up the skies. Well, they sent her

82

back home in a nice wooden box…they'd read that nice eulogy about her nicks and knocks. But they didn't say anything that put her childhood at fault… and that's what she slipped on to fall. I heard she flew to the moon, on a bright summer's day… but she flew way too close and she wanted so to stay! But they locked her up tight for a daydream or two... And that's when they asked her…"Who are you?" I heard she's still Azure Blue.

...

In wisps of golden years he stands
beneath the haloed sunlit bands;
as winter sneaks past youth, it blows,
to rise once more and fall as snow.

There's so much more for him to see
before he sleeps eternally;
as in and out his breath will flow,
to rise once more and fall as snow.

Though life is mostly lived by youth,
and older men don't know the truth;
That when they face the end, they glow
and rise once more to fall as snow.

He misses her, now twenty years,
and though time's healed his wounds and fears
he's ready now, he wants to go
to rise once more and fall as snow.

...

Out here, in solitude
there's something I need-
a chance to be still
in peaceful retreat

Free from cacophonous
pounding of drums
free to sit silent
in stillness- become.

Touch souls with nature
seek out my peace
inside, earth's quiet
awakens in me

the will to go on
    a balance I need

When the world loses theirs
it will live on in me.

...

Build me an ocean of raindrops,
a bottle of sand-covered tears;
hold me forever in daydreams
through all of our whimsical years.

Sleep sweet moose on my shoulder,
in a forest of newly felled leaves;
the winter creeps in as you hold her,
but only if your heart believes.

Toss out a life ring to save me
past my heart-bleeding fears;
swim in those leaves while heartbroken,
as I wrap you in love while you're here.

We are the makers of daydreams,
we are the savers of souls,
stay by my side; lonely days, lonely nights
promise we'll grow to be old.

...

I am that old tree
Alone on the hill
I wave at the ocean
Feeling the thrill

Of a life that's lived long
And lived well on the edge
As my Sticky stark limbs
Rise from my chest

I embark each new sunrise
Stretch limbs in the air
Call to the oceans
And the mermaids out there

I will pull from the earth
While I'm able to stand
Then fall to my knees
And nurture the land

In my last breath, lie heaving
Out oxygen sighs
To the next generation
And my final sunrise

Until then, I stand proudly
My roots in the land
Til the wind sweeps my last breath
Cross the cool ocean sand

...

Art is...

Soothing a beast that's within me
Letting my vision see light
Stroking the air with my soul in my hands
Giving my fantasies life.

Salving a wound that needs healing
Cut and still bleeding me out
Finding its way to the surface somehow
Feeling a real need to shout

Busting at seams to be seen by
Those who will let it sink in
Knowing perhaps it might fall at my feet
Each piece can't possibly get in!

Subdued in my mouth and restrained now
By society's wintery glove
Breaking the ice in distress to just breathe
But cooled by its pure, healing love.

...

When darkness takes over
just before light
as a calmness approaches my chair

The wind whispers softly
into the pale light
"Be still, and know I am there."

...

Against a dismal sky of gray it grows
A beauty in my younger days before,
I climbed it daily in my youth, and so
As I grew daily seemed to need it more

I'd rest upon the branches way up high
Just sit amongst the leaves so lovely green
To watch the birds or wanderers go by
And quietly I'd sit and not be seen

This tree in majesty grew branches wide
Our secrets we would keep with pinky swears
It's shade would make a place for us to hide
"Til death," we'd promise, sealed, and with a glare

The years passed by and we all grew apart
Our lives moved on and we, separate ways
As I came home to mend my broken heart
It fell upon its bed... I cried that day

We so remembered, and we so recalled
The times we played amongst its charming arms
To me the tree was love and that was all
I could not bear to see it in such harm

I knelt beside the place where it once stood
And growing there, a tiny plant, a tree!
I had begun to cry, I knew I would...
I knelt beside the sapling in the leaves

Beneath the lovely tree had grown one more
I turned my crying eyes toward the sky
I smiled at Heaven, for I knew the score
And turning 'round, said quietly, "goodbye"

I wonder about the trees that were around
our home, they used to make a *crishing* sound;
       each leaf, a song of its own-
       singing out to children,
       and to their children-
            to their own.

Finding a way to say to them,
       "Someday, you'll see.
       You'll look around,
       then, not a sound...
       yes, you'll wonder, about me."

That last tree in its wisdom standing tall
among the clouds, high
       sang loudly, that day-
       piercing the winter sky.

Now, thirty years later...
I look across this quarry
at what they mean;
     the hillsides bare...
     the smog-covered air...

       not a sound...
       not a tree.

Inspiration: First line of Robert Frost's, "The Sound of Trees"

…

I was a sapling, a handsome young oak;
I bore those sweet sprouts from the base of my trunk!

Content in my vastness, I'd sprout up, push out,
bending and twisting; rising through the air!

Tearing past clouds, looming over fences,
wild with abandon, stretching out my arms!
I was the mightiest of trees, yes I was,

but, even the fittest may fall…

Now I am that dead tree, but don't weep for me,
for I may return-
With time and affection,
        some sweet resurrection…
        with godspeed, one more seed
I may grow.

...

Crisp fingers clutching wintry sky
as grey clouds skitter
skulking by
past seasons on southern soft sighs
garbles of geese amble on-
      -- reasons for the season
      now gone-

Memories fly past cans
stuffed with trappings of packages,
ribbons and wrappings
jammed tight from stacking.

Men, dauntingly dusted,
downright disgusted,
drive by in trucks;
jaws musty from busting
boxes and bags,
trimmings and tags-
leftover happenings of seasonal snags

Day-after
Martyr's death of the season
thrown out the tree
yet what was the reason?

Lights flicker, die
along with the season...

and the snow.

Crisp fingers clutch wintry sky,
grey clouds gather,
skulking by-

seasons pass,
soft southern sigh…
garbling geese amble on-

another winter,
gone.

...

I am that dead tree with sticky stark limbs
who pokes at the blue skies all day
raging at heaven for killing my soul
then, leaving my roots here in clay!

I may be a dead tree who stands so erectly-
a blackened, decaying, crisp shell-
but one who reaches and stretches
to all points...

just to get farther from hell.

I'm the one who has sucked from the earth,
all I can- one who had nothing to lose...
one who'll return to the loam where I stand,
in the bottomless pit where I grew.

I'm now a dead tree, but I once was so green,
my shoots grew so quickly, and free!
Yes, I was alive, with sheen on my leaves,
my suppleness shined; how I thrived!

...

Each time a candle burns I think,
I see your spirit flicker there.
My faith too often on the brink-
it wanders as I wonder... where?

Your life, just like that candle dear,
burned out too soon and left me here.
I'll roam this lonely world below
and wonder, as I wander, though...

...

As water rushes past
The creeks will rise
As too, your memory,
Inside my eyes
When hummingbirds
and blue jays
Take to flight
Another moon of June
Inside me, dies
      The boy I knew
      has flown to other skies
      The things they say of heaven,
      Are they lies?

Without you here
I seem to be weighed down
The hope just gropes
And tries to crush my crown
No more my brother's mother
Seems to laugh
And time for rhyme,
it seems, has surely passed

So fly on Curt, the earth
Remembers you
The clouds so loud
Rush past as if they knew
The loss I feel subdues my joy,
but then
Someday, my brother,
I hope we'll meet again

...

My blue jay flies
In sunny skies
Or misty days
When tearful cries
Of missing you
Escape my eyes
Reminds me when
Our laughter rang
As blue jays flew
And joyful, sang
Outside our window
Now, just mine,
He sits and chirps
It seems a sign
He drops a feather
As I cry
Reminds me of
our love, and I
Know we will meet
someday up high
Until that time;
My blue jay flies

...

Now he flies with hummingbirds
against a gentle wind
Trapped no more inside himself
He's free to fly again

His spirit soars amongst the stars
and though we're left to grieve—
His soul will fly with hummingbirds
as long as we believe!

For Curt

Acknowledgements

*I would like to acknowledge the person who made this book
come to fruition; my son, Landon Ginn. Thank you for
pushing this book upstream so that my dream of being a
published poet finally come true at the age of 60.*

*To my husband, Jimmy Ginn; I love you beyond measure.
Thank you for sticking with me for forty years and
counting, always supporting me and my art. You are my
rock.*

*To my daughter, Skye, who is the undisputed Diamond of
my Uterus. I adore you and I thank you for inspiring so
many poems (even if you had no idea that you did).*

*To my mother, Faye Schroeder who continues to be my role
model and the light which guides my way.*

*To my dear sister, Chris, and my brother, Curt (who we lost
too soon)… thank you for never saying my poetry sucked,
even when it did.*

*To my best friend, Da Mutt, who always believes that
everything I touch turns to gold, and to my dear friend,
Nicole, who always gets me… I'm glad we both survived.*

*To my F…armerz; I'm alive because of you. Finally, to
every dog we've had through the years; thank for sharing
the late nights debating with me which words to use. I
couldn't have done it without you.*

Biography

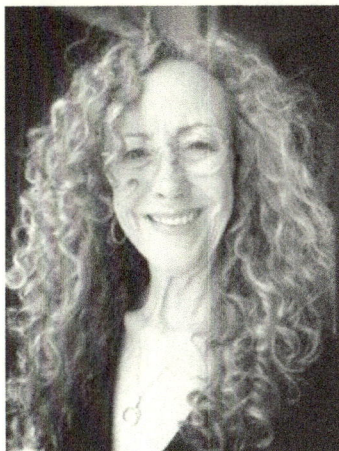

Cat S. Ginn (Catherine Schroeder Ginn) is a poet, artist, and lover of words. She was born in the south, moving around quite a bit, before ending up in southeast Oklahoma at the age of eleven. After having earned her BS in Art/Marketing she married and moved to Louisiana and Alaska before settling in Texas in 1992.

Cat is an introvert who finds solace in quiet moments; writing, drawing, and talking to her dogs (or any dog, really). She looks to the moon, the trees, the ocean, the wind, and inside herself for words to share with anyone who will read or listen. This is her first book (thanks to the motivation of her son, Landon) and she has been dreaming of this moment for most of her life. Cat has written thousands of poems, spent countless nights writing, drawing and painting; and a good majority of the last decade renovating her home. In the past, she has learned from many poets all over the world on fanstory.com and won many awards. She earned the title of #2 poet two years running as *I am Cat*. Since leaving the site she has been working on compiling her poetry, relaxing by the pool, and is often caught staring into nothingness. She's been married to the same man for nearly forty years, has two grown children, two attention-seeking dogs, and three spoiled grand dogs. She lives a few doors down from her best friend and can finally say she's found peace in her life.

Made in the USA
Las Vegas, NV
07 March 2022